MAINSTREAMING GENDER IN THE CONTROL OF SMALL ARMS AND LIGHT WEAPONS

Baudouin Ngah Akoh

Table of Content

INTRODUCTION

The proliferation of Small Arms and Light Weapons (SALW) is a global challenge, responsible for a staggering number of deaths, human rights violations, and ongoing conflicts. Viewing these lethal tools through a purely security-focused lens may obscure the critical gender-specific dimensions of their impact. Hence, this paper seeks to illuminate the intricate relationship between SALW and sexual and gender-based violence (SGBV). We recognize that the consequences of SALW reach far beyond the immediate battlefield, profoundly influencing both men and women across various social contexts. The paper has three main sections.

Section 1 establishes the foundation by providing a comprehensive overview of the global landscape of SALW, shedding light on its devastating effects and underscoring the urgent need for a more inclusive approach to SALW control. This section draws attention to the gendered impact of SALW, where women and men experience the effects of these weapons differently, often with women disproportionately affected by gender-based violence.

Section 2 explores the crucial aspects of mainstreaming gender considerations into SALW control. It emphasizes the need for gender-sensitive legislation and regulations, as well as the importance of gender-sensitive training for stakeholders in SALW control efforts. Recognizing that progress has been made, but challenges remain, this section underscores the significance of integrating gender perspectives into policy and legislation to address gender-based violence effectively.

Section 3 examines compelling case studies that underscore the gender-specific dimensions of SALW control. From post-conflict regions to South East Europe, South Africa, and Serbia, these cases offer valuable insights into the impact of SALW on both men and women and the strategies and challenges in mainstreaming gender considerations into SALW control.

Together, these sections aim to provide a holistic understanding of the complex and multifaceted relationship between SALW and gender dynamics. This paper underscores the pressing need to mainstream gender considerations in SALW control policies, hoping that the insights gleaned from these sections will inform and inspire efforts to create a more equitable and secure world, where the gender-specific impacts of small arms and light weapons are effectively addressed.

1. GENDERED DIMENSIONS OF SMALL ARMS AND LIGHT WEAPONS PROLIFERATION AND USE

The proliferation and use of SALW have long been recognized as complex and multifaceted phenomena, involving the intersections of a myriad of actors, motivations, and consequences. In the midst of these intersections, a cocktail of gendered dimensions emerges, shaping the experiences of various segments of society, including women, men, the elderly, children, and individuals with disabilities. These gender dynamics influence the ways in which different individuals are affected by violence, displacement, and the broader repercussions of weapon use. It is evident that the availability and use of SALW play a crucial role in exacerbating conflicts and pains, leaving indelible marks on the hearts and lives of those involved.

This section explores the intricate interplay between gender and SALW, seeking to shed light on the far-reaching consequences of their presence in conflict settings. We begin by examining the findings and insights provided by Conaway (2012), who offers a comprehensive overview of how SALW proliferation intertwines with gender dynamics in conflict zones. Further, we examine the gendered attitudes towards SALW, shedding light on the disparities in access and impact that different gender groups experience. This includes the societal ideologies that underpin these differences, contributing to the perpetuation of violence, particularly against women and girls. The overarching challenge we address in this section is the imperative to mainstream gender considerations in SALW control efforts. Despite the prevalence of the rhetoric of 'gender mainstreaming' in international agreements, the actual implementation of policies that ensure equal attention to the needs and experiences of women and men remains an uphill struggle. We examine the existing international frameworks related to SALW control, such as the United Nations Program of Action (POA) on SALW, the Arms Trade Treaty (ATT), and the UN Security Council Resolutions on Women, Peace, and Security (WPS). While these agreements lay the groundwork for addressing the gendered impact of SALW, practical strategies for their implementation require ongoing attention and reinforcement.

The gendered impact of SALW proliferation is the most devastating consequence, particularly concerning violence against women and girls. By exploring these gendered dimensions of SALW proliferation, we aim to contribute to a more comprehensive understanding of the challenges posed by these weapons and the necessity of integrating gender perspectives into SALW control efforts.

Gendered Dimensions of SALW Availability and Use

Armed conflicts often have gendered dimensions, with women, men, the elderly, children, and physically challenged persons experiencing the conflicts differently. Women/girls can be more vulnerable to certain forms of violence, including sexual violence and displacement, while more men than women are directly involved in combat. The availability and use of Small Arms and Light Weapons (SALW) exacerbate these gender disparities. Conaway (2012) summarizes the dimensions of SALW proliferation:

- Women and girls face higher risks of sexual and gender-based violence in conflict settings where SALW are used as tools of war. Displacement caused by SALW-related violence may lead to additional vulnerabilities, including losing access to healthcare, education, and economic opportunities.
- Traditional gender roles and power dynamics often intersect with SALW proliferation. In many societies, men have greater access to and control over SALW,

reinforcing existing gender inequalities and creating an environment where violence is used to exert control.

· In conflicts where women participate as combatants or members of armed groups, gender dynamics can shape their involvement. Understanding female combatants' motivations, experiences, and roles is essential for developing appropriate disarmament and reintegration programs.

Gender Differences in Attitudes towards SALW

Conaway (2012) further explains common gendered differences in attitude towards SALW as follows:

· Anecdotal evidence suggests that women, men, and children do not have equal access to SALW and are differently affected by their misuse during and after conflicts.

·   Experts suggest a possible link between 'everyday' violence and the 'unspeakable' extremes of violence in conflict situations. These links are primarily supported by gender ideologies that uphold and glorify male superiority and condone male aggression toward women and children.

·   Guns are hazardous when kept at home. Evidence points to the fact that having firearms at home increases their chances of being used recklessly.

·   A man causing harm to his female partner is not considered as an unthinkable act. Quite often, society can understand it as an outcome of provocation, especially if infidelity is suspected. Such attitudes, even among legal authorities, result in lenient sentences and perpetuate violence against women.

·   Although more men than women die due to firearms, the easy availability of SALW perpetuates male dominance and facilitates violence against women in conflict zones. However, it is wrong to depict women solely as victims and men solely as perpetrators. In some cultures, women uphold the belief that their male partners need guns for protection, and in others, women engage directly in armed violence as perpetrators. Such attitudes reveal that women cannot always be characterized as inherently peace-loving and fundamentally opposed to the presence and use of arms.

The Challenge of Gender Mainstreaming in SALW Control

The rhetoric of 'gender mainstreaming' has permeated international agreements, but practical strategies to ensure equal attention to women and men have been difficult to implement. The proliferation of SALW, ease of use, and lethal impact necessitate gender-aware policies, research, and activism. Although international agreements like the Beijing Platform of Action, the Windhoek Declaration, and Resolution 1325 provide formal avenues to hold governments and international agencies accountable for addressing gender-based violence perpetuated by small arms, the political will to implement them needs continuing strengthening (NATO, u.d; Conaway, 2012; UNFPA, 2002). The gendered impact of SALW remains the most devastating consequence of its proliferation, particularly in the context of violence against women and girls (Watson, 2022). The various dimensions of SALW on the well-being of women/girls are explained further below.

Impact on Physical and Psychological Well-being

Direct and Indirect Harm: The presence and use of SALW in conflict zones and areas of insecurity lead to physical and psychological harm to women and girls. Direct harm includes injuries and fatalities from gun violence, including indiscriminate attacks, shelling, and sniper fire. Indirect harm encompasses the consequences of displacement, loss of livelihoods, and disruptions in healthcare and education services due to armed violence.

Trauma and Psychological Distress: Women and girls exposed to SALW violence often suffer psychological trauma and distress. Witnessing the wanton destruction of property, losing loved ones, and experiencing sexual and gender-based violence can cause long-lasting mental health issues, including post-traumatic stress disorder and depression.

Fear and Insecurity: The widespread availability of SALW creates a climate of fear and insecurity within communities, especially for women and girls. They may feel vulnerable to sexual violence and other forms of gender-based violence, leading to self-imposed restrictions on their movements and activities, further limiting their agency and autonomy.

GBV as a Weapon of War

Instrument of Control: GBV, often perpetrated using SALW, is a weapon of war in conflict settings. Armed groups and militias use sexual violence, forced marriages, and other forms of abuse to control populations, instill fear, and maintain dominance.

Forced Displacement: The threat of GBV, including sexual violence, can lead to the forced displacement of women and girls. They may flee their homes to escape the immediate danger, becoming internally displaced or seeking refuge in other countries. This displacement exacerbates vulnerabilities and disrupts their lives.

Reproductive Health and Family Structure: Sexual violence associated with SALW conflicts can result in unwanted pregnancies and sexually transmitted infections, including HIV. It can also lead to the breakdown of family structures and the stigmatization of survivors, further complicating post-conflict recovery.

Long-Term Consequences: The impact of gender-based violence as a weapon can have enduring effects on survivors, their families, and their communities, hindering recovery and reconciliation processes.

Access to SALW Reinforces Traditional Power Dynamics

Historical Gender Roles: The availability and control of SALW have historically reinforced these roles, often with men as the primary beneficiaries of access to these weapons, sustaining their position of power and authority.

Control of Resources and Decision-Making: In many societies, men predominantly control access to resources, including weapons. The control over SALW can influence decision-making processes related to conflict, security, and community affairs, leaving women marginalized and with limited influence over such matters.

Armed Groups and Gender Dynamics: Power dynamics are often heavily gendered within armed groups and militias. Women are typically underrepresented in leadership roles and are rarely involved in decision-making processes regarding the acquisition, use, and control of SALW. This underrepresentation of women reinforces traditional gender hierarchies and power imbalances.

Women's Limited Access to Self-Defense

Legal and Cultural Barriers: Societal norms and restrictive firearms laws can hinder women's ability to protect themselves in situations of violence, leaving them more vulnerable to harm.

Resource Constraints: Women often face economic constraints that make it difficult to access and own SALW for self-defense. The cost of purchasing firearms, obtaining licenses, and undergoing training can be prohibitive for many women, limiting their ability to defend themselves.

Limited Training Opportunities: Women may need more opportunities to effectively acquire the skills and knowledge necessary to use SALW for self-defense. This lack of training can render any access to SALW less impactful.

 Women who seek to defend themselves with SALW may face social stigmatization and victim-blaming, which can dissuade them from taking measures to protect themselves, as they may fear social consequences or legal repercussions.

Existing International Frameworks for SALW Control

Joshi (n.d), UNIDIR (2020), and International Action Network on Small Arms (2021) offer detailed reviews of the key international agreements and conventions related to SALW control, which are summarized below:

United Nations Program of Action on SALW (UNPoA): Adopted in 2001, the UNPoA provides a comprehensive framework for addressing the illicit trade in SALW. It encourages states to take measures to strengthen national controls, enhance cooperation on arms transfers, and promote transparency. Although the UNPoA does not explicitly focus on gender, it recognizes the importance of addressing the humanitarian impact of SALW, which includes GBV and harm to women/girls.

The International Tracing Instrument (ITI): The ITI, developed as part of the UNPoA, provides guidelines for marking and tracing SALW. Effective tracing mechanisms can help identify the sources of illicit weapons, combat arms trafficking, and ensure accountability. Although the ITI does not explicitly address gender, it indirectly contributes to conflict prevention and reducing GBV.

Sustainable Development Goal (SDG) 16: SDG 16 – on peace, justice, and strong institutions, and its Target 16.4, calls for a significant reduction in illicit arms flows, with achievement depending on the whole and effective implementation of the PoA and ITI.

Arms Trade Treaty (ATT): The ATT, established in 2014, seeks to regulate international trade in conventional arms, including SALW, to prevent their diversion to unauthorized users and minimize human suffering. While gender is not explicitly mentioned in the treaty, GBV and the humanitarian consequences of the arms trade are relevant issues addressed within its scope.

UN Security Council Resolutions on Women, Peace, and Security: A series of UN Security Council Resolutions (UNSCRs) known as the Women, Peace, and Security (WPS) agenda, including UNSCR 1325 and subsequent resolutions, emphasize the importance of women's participation in conflict prevention and resolution, as well as the need to address the gender-specific impact of armed conflicts. These resolutions call for more significant consideration of gender perspectives in all peace and security efforts, including SALW control.

The Geneva Declaration on Armed Violence and Development: This multi-stakeholder initiative, launched in 2008, focuses on preventing and reducing armed violence and promoting development. The Geneva

Declaration recognizes the gendered dimensions of armed violence and underscores the need for gender-sensitive approaches to SALW control.

The Nairobi Protocol on Small Arms and Light Weapons: This regional instrument, adopted in 2000 by the member states of the Intergovernmental Authority on Development (IGAD), focuses on SALW control in the East African region. While not a global framework, it emphasizes the importance of addressing gender-based violence and the need for a gender perspective in SALW control.

These international frameworks, while not all explicitly gender-focused, lay the groundwork for addressing the gendered impact of SALW and the importance of integrating gender perspectives into SALW control efforts, and they call for the consideration of the humanitarian and human rights aspects of SALW. Recognizing the connections between SALW, gender, peace, and security is a vital step in promoting a more comprehensive and inclusive approach to addressing the challenges posed by these weapons (United States Institute of Peace, n.d.).

Additionally, the Human Rights Council regularly addresses the impact of arms transfers on human rights, particularly regarding civilian acquisition, possession, and use of firearms. Also, UNODA actively promotes the comprehensive integration of gender perspectives into all aspects of SALW control. Moreover, states must report their implementation commitments under the PoA and ITI. These commitments span various themes, including national coordination agencies, manufacturing, marking, record-keeping, tracing, international transfers, brokering, stockpile management, surplus, public awareness, confidence-building, and more. Although many countries submit their reports online, these reports are rarely verified or assessed for actual implementation. Many countries need proper weapons marking upon import, maintain records for the stipulated time, have less regulated internal transit channels, and help understand and address brokering issues (Bonn International Center for Conversion, n.d.).

2. INTEGRATING GENDER PERSPECTIVES INTO SALW CONTROL POLICY AND LEGISLATION

This section discusses the critical theme of integrating gender perspectives into SALW control policy and legislation, underscoring the pivotal role that comprehensive policy frameworks and gender-sensitive training play in addressing the gender-specific impact of small arms and light weapons. By doing so, it seeks to create a more just, equitable, and inclusive approach to security and peacebuilding.

The section opens with an exploration of the two fundamental aspects involved in integrating gender perspectives into SALW control efforts. The first aspect focuses on the development of gender-sensitive legislation and regulations, providing the legal foundation to ensure accountability for perpetrators and support for survivors of gender-based violence. The second aspect pertains to gender-sensitive training, which equips stakeholders with the knowledge and skills necessary to effectively implement these legal frameworks. Such training includes addressing domestic and sexual violence in conflict and post-conflict situations.

Integrating gender perspectives into SALW control has garnered increased attention in recent years, as the small arms control agenda converges with international policies on gender equality and women's empowerment. We highlight several notable instances of this alignment, including the Sustainable Development Goals (SDG) 16 on peace and SDG 5 on gender equality, as well as key international agreements like the Convention on the Elimination of All Forms of Discrimination Against Women (CEDAW) and the Beijing Declaration. Initiatives such as the Spotlight Initiative further emphasize the urgency of addressing the intersection of gender equality, women's empowerment, and SALW control. Also discussed in this section is the United Nations Development Program's (UNDP) comprehensive eight-point agenda for gender equality in crisis prevention. The UNDP's eight-point agenda encompasses security, justice, leadership, disaster risk reduction, recovery, governance, and societal transformation.

Another critical aspect discussed in this section is the incorporation of a gender perspective into situational analysis, ensuring that gender considerations permeate the entire project or program development process. By collecting sex-disaggregated data, addressing the roles, needs, and participation of women, men, girls, and boys, and avoiding the reinforcement of gender stereotypes, projects and programs become more inclusive and equitable. How women's NGOs can drive transformative changes in community perceptions and contribute to equitable structural changes within families and communities is also discussed. Furthermore, we expand the discussion to encompass emerging weapon technologies, such as cybersecurity, artificial intelligence, and weapons of mass destruction, and their potential gendered impacts, recognizing the need to address these intersections of gender perspectives and security concerns exhaustively.

Generally, integrating gender perspectives into policy and legislation involves two essential aspects: developing gender-sensitive legislation and regulations and promoting gender-sensitive training. The first part involves putting in place the legal frameworks that ensure that perpetrators are held accountable while the survivors receive support and protection. The second part involves disseminating information about the legal framework and training the relevant stakeholders on their respective roles and how and when to apply them. In particular, training should include identifying and responding to domestic and sexual violence in conflict and post-conflict situations. UNODA notes that progress has been made, but few member states have fully incorporated gender considerations into PoA implementation, including collecting sex-disaggregated data (UNODA, u.d).

Convergence of Small Arms Control Agenda with International Policies on Gender Equality and Women Empowerment

Recent years have witnessed the convergence of the small arms control agenda with international policies on gender equality and women's empowerment (Bastick, n.d.). A few notable points to support this viewpoint are explained briefly below:

1. SDG 16 on peace, security, and strong institutions is particularly relevant to small arms control, while SDG 5 is on gender equality and women's empowerment (UN, 2022).

2. The Convention on the Elimination of All Forms of Discrimination Against Women (CEDAW) and the Beijing Declaration provide a strong normative basis for aligning the Women, Peace, and Security (WPS) and small arms control agendas. Initiatives like the Spotlight Initiative to eliminate violence against

women and girls further emphasize the urgency of addressing this issue.

3.   Between 2019 and 2022, UNODA implemented a global project to support gender mainstreaming in policies, programs, and actions against SALW trafficking and misuse, aligning with the Women, Peace, and Security (WPS) agenda and funded by the European Union. The follow-on project, extending until 2025, strengthens states' capacity for gender-responsive SALW control policies and programs (UNODA, u.d).

4.   The WPS agenda and the SDGs are being aligned to reshape the gendered dimension of insecurity. This shift broadens discussions from technical, security-focused perspectives to encompass human security concerns like gender equality and women's empowerment (OSCE, u.d).

By integrating gender perspectives into policy and legislation and promoting gender-sensitive training for security forces, SALW control efforts can become more effective in addressing the gender-specific impact of these weapons. Such measures are crucial for preventing and responding to gender-based violence and promoting a more inclusive and equitable approach to security and peacebuilding. Engendering SALW usage and control goes to show that gender mainstreaming in SALW control is both a matter of compliance and an imperative for achieving comprehensive, just, and lasting peace (UN, 2006; LeBrun, 2019).

UNDP Ten-Point Agenda for Gender Equality in Crisis Prevention

UNDP (2022) provides an eight-point agenda for gender equality in crisis prevention which is summarized below:

> 1. Strengthening women's security in crisis by ending VAW/G.
> 2. Advancing gender justice by ensuring justice and security for women

3.   Expanding women's citizenship, participation, and leadership, by empowering women as decision-makers.

4.   Building peace with and for women by involving women in all peace processes.

5.   Promoting gender equality in disaster risk reduction by supporting women and men to rebuild better.

6.   Ensuring gender-responsive recovery by empowering women as recovery leaders.

7.   Transforming government to deliver for women by including women's issues in the national agenda

8.   Developing capacities for social change by collaborating to transform society.

UNDP (2022) submits that the following has to be done to achieve this Eight-Point Agenda:

a.   Support full implementation of Security Council Resolution 1325.

b.   Incorporate gender equality priorities into advocacy and strategic planning in development, humanitarian, peace, and security.

c.   Strengthen human resources, policies, and programs for responsiveness and accountability on gender issues.

d.   Build partnerships to maximize impact on gender priorities.

e.   Develop gender-responsive funding mechanisms and resource mobilization strategies.

f.   Support data collection that focuses on women's perspectives and values.

g.   Advance intellectual leadership, knowledge management, and monitoring and evaluation of gender and crisis prevention and recovery (CPR) issues.

Incorporating Gender Perspective in Situational Analysis

UNODC (2020) explains why and how to incorporate a gender perspective into the situational analysis. Engendering situation analyses ensure that gender considerations permeate the design of the program/project, encompassing the results framework, activities, and indicators. An engendered situation analysis necessitates using sex-disaggregated data and guarantees that development projects and programs account for the roles, needs, and participation of women, men, girls, and boys. When formulating the project/program, it is crucial to keep these general questions in mind:

1. Include a gender expert on the assessment/formulation team, incorporate gender issues during information gathering and analysis, and ensure that the respondents are sufficiently representative of the different gender groups.

2. Ensure that the questioning is inclusive of the different gender groups.

3. Take into account the policy and legal framework and critical issues related to gender equality and women empowerment.

Addressing Gender Issues

In addressing gender issues:

· Give special preference to underrepresented individuals, ensuring their equal benefit from the project.

· Ensure project/program alignment with the UN commitments on gender equality and women's empowerment, and does not exacerbate existing inequalities.

· Use gender-sensitive language in project resources, reports, and promotions, and avoid reinforcing gender stereotypes in the project's IEC materials.

· Utilize data and indicators highlighting different needs and interests based on sex, sexual orientation, sex characteristics, and gender identity.

This comprehensive approach to gender mainstreaming will help ensure that gender considerations are integrated throughout the project/program development process, from the initial situational analysis to the implementation phase (UNDP 2022).

The Rise of Women's NGOs in Post-Conflict Settings

To support the campaign for mainstreaming of gender in SALW control, numerous women's NGOs have emerged at local and international levels. Their efforts encompass empowering women, fostering democratic practices, building inter-ethnic trust through community projects, forming coalitions and partnerships with civil society groups, and engaging in reproductive health activities among other pro-women and children's efforts (Reaching Critical Will of the Women's International League for Peace and Freedom, 2016). Women's NGOs face several challenges, including the absence of established NGO legislation, communication difficulties with governments and local authorities, and inadequate national and international outreach for effective conflict responses. Despite these constraints, women's NGOs drive transformative changes in community perceptions and reinforce equitable structural changes within families and communities (UNFPA, 2002).

GBV Issues in Refugee Camps

Recent international events have brought issues of GBV among refugees and the internally displaced, and post-conflict scenarios to public attention. Humanitarian organizations increasingly recognize that GBV violates public health principles, universal human rights, and the recovery of refugee and internally displaced families and communities. However, tools for addressing gender-based violence in conflict and post-conflict settings are limited, and the humanitarian community's capacity to address it comprehensively is inadequate. There are no standardized methods for assessing the effectiveness of international and local NGO programs, and there is limited data on the prevalence of gender-based violence and best practices for assessment (UNFPA, 2002).

Expanding Gender Perspectives: Cybersecurity, Artificial Intelligence, and Weapons of Mass Destruction

UNIDIR (2020) explores the relevance of gender perspectives in the context of other emerging weapon technologies, such as the potential gendered impacts of cyberattacks on critical infrastructure, such as hospitals, which could disproportionately affect pregnant and nursing women. Less developed countries seeking to enhance their cyber capabilities face challenges related to the cost of cybersecurity infrastructure, the absence of early warning systems, and shortages of cyber professionals. In particular, African countries rely on imported cyber technology, leaving them potentially vulnerable to cyber threats. There is also the campaign against autonomous weapons systems, known as "Stop Killer Robots," which can select, track, and engage targets without human intervention. There are also concerns regarding the gendered impacts of nuclear and biological weapons. Recent discussions addressing nuclear weapons have acknowledged the disproportionate impact of ionizing radiation on the health of women and girls. Drawing from the Ebola epidemic, there is fear that weaponized diseases could impact women and men differently, as women often bear the responsibility for providing care and handling burial practices.

3. CASE STUDIES OF MAINSTREAMING SEXUAL AND GENDER-BASED VIOLENCE IN SALW CONTROL

In this section, we present a series of insightful case studies that underscore the intricate relationship between SALW and SGBV. These case studies offer valuable lessons and insights into the gender-specific dimensions of SALW control. They also reveal that the impact of SALW extends beyond traditional conflict scenarios and affects the security and well-being of both men and women in diverse social contexts. Through these case studies, we aim to shed light on the complex and multifaceted relationship between SALW and SGBV, emphasizing the importance of mainstreaming gender considerations in SALW control and drawing attention to the unique challenges and opportunities present in post-conflict regions, Southeast East Europe, South Africa, and Serbia.

These case studies collectively underscore the necessity of gender-responsive policies, data collection, and advocacy to address the gender-specific impacts of SALW effectively.

Case Study 1: Sexual and Gender-Based Violence in Post-Conflict Regions - the Case of Bosnia and Herzegovina

Post-conflict regions have the advantage of nurturing civil society and cultivating innovative ideas and capacities, in contrast to the situation under a full-scale war.

Torture in Concentration Camps

Men As Victims of Sexual and Gender-Based Abuse: The torture endured in some concentration camps affected more men than women. For instance, in the Sarajevo Canton, of the 6,000 concentration camp victims, 5,000 were men, with an alarming 80 percent of them reportedly experiencing rape. Unfortunately, little attention has been given to men who, like women, are victims of sexual violence.

Women Are Not Always Passive and Peaceful: A common assumption, based on feminist thought that men are inherently aggressive and violent while women are passive and peaceful is universally correct. In the Balkan region, several women supported the war but did so differently from their partners directly involved in the conflict. For instance, in 1991, the image of Serbian women cheering on their husbands, sons, brothers, and fathers heading to fight in Croatia remained a potent and enduring memory of the war. Conversely, Serbian women who protested the war at Belgrade's central square represent another vivid image.

Men are Not Exclusively Pro-Conflict: The notion that men are exclusively pro-conflict is also challenged historically, as male soldiers often had the most to lose in conflicts. During conflicts in the Balkan region, many men, particularly young men, fled their countries to avoid fighting. In Serbia, defectors are labeled ethnic traitors, the most severe stigma in Serbian culture. In Bosnia and Herzegovina, defectors are frequently blocklisted, making it challenging to secure employment and subjecting them to verbal abuse.

A clear message from the Bosnia and Herzegovina case is that it is wrong to equate GBV to violence against women/girls as though they are synonymous; men/boys are sometimes victims of sexual violence. Also, women can be perpetrators and supporters of SALW proliferation and use.

Case Study 2: Main Gender Concerns Related to SALW in South East Europe

In 2016, SEESAC conducted a comprehensive study on Gender and SALW in South East Europe with the following objectives:

- Identify gender concerns related to SALW in South East Europe.

·	Assess the integration of the gender perspective into SALW policies in the region, including legislative and strategic frameworks.

·	Provide evidence-based recommendations and practical tools for incorporating the gender perspective into SALW legislative and strategic frameworks.

The Key Findings

The analysis of sex-disaggregated data collected in collaboration with SALW Commissions confirmed that dominant gender patterns significantly influence SALW practices and their consequences (OSCE, u.d; UNWomen, n.d.). Specifically:

·	Men overwhelmingly dominate firearm ownership (over 95%).

·	Men constitute the majority of perpetrators (98%) and victims (83%) of firearm-related incidents.

· Women rarely act as perpetrators (2%) but are more frequently victims (17%).

· Firearms in domestic violence incidents disproportionately affect women, with intimate partner homicide being a common form of women's homicide.

· The high lethality of firearms in domestic violence incidents is a significant concern.

· Young men are disproportionately involved in firearm-related incidents.

· Women tend to hold more negative views about SALW and often advocate for stricter regulations.

· Women are underrepresented in policymaking and institutions related to SALW control.

Based on these findings, SEESAC conducted a comprehensive gender analysis of SALW control strategies, action plans, firearm laws, and related documents in Southeast Europe (SEESAC, 2018). The main findings include:

1.   Gender issues are under-prioritized in SALW control policy/programs. Hence, policies in South East Europe do not adequately address gender issues.

2.   Legislation primarily focuses on domestic violence, with provisions restricting firearm access in domestic violence cases. However, the number of women killed with firearms within domestic contexts remains high.

3.   Lack of sex-disaggregated data and comprehensive research hinders gender-responsive SALW policies.

4.   Gender analysis is generally absent from policymaking processes, making gender concerns about SALW invisible or only sporadically addressed.

The study concluded that SALW legislative and strategic frameworks in Southeast Europe overlooked gender differences in ownership, use, and misuse of firearms and the differentiated impacts of firearms on women and men. This gender-blind approach leads to persistent problems, such as intimate partner femicide and the overrepresentation of young men among perpetrators and victims, that cannot be effectively addressed without mainstreaming gender considerations (OSCE, u.d; UNWomen, n.d.).

Case Study 3: Gender and Small Arms Policymaking in South Africa

South Africa stands out among non-conflict-affected countries for its high prevalence of lethal violence against women and girls, including a high female homicide rate, widespread sexual and gender-based violence (GBV), and a significant cost associated with GBV. These issues are exacerbated by socioeconomic inequality, cultural norms that accept violence, weak law enforcement, and children's exposure to violence, leading to a cycle of violence. Gun use and violence in South Africa have complex gender dimensions. While most legal gun owners are men, most firearms are registered for self-defense purposes, and men over 50 constitute the largest demographic of gun owners (UNWomen, n.d.).

The enactment of the FCA occurred in 2000, shortly after South Africa marked the end of apartheid. This transition led to the introduction of progressive laws, including a new constitution (1996) and legislation addressing women's concerns and well-being, such as the Choice on Termination of Pregnancy Act of 1996 and the Domestic Violence Act (DVA) of 1998. Elements of the FCA also reflected this gender focus by considering domestic violence incidents as grounds for firearm license refusal. The Act also empowered courts and law enforcement agencies to remove firearms from individuals misusing them, particularly in domestic violence cases. Additionally, the DVA allowed women to report the presence of firearms in domestic violence incidents or when seeking domestic violence protection orders at magistrates' courts.

Gun Violence Perpetrators and Victims in South Africa

Most gun violence victims are young black men living in urban areas and victimized by other young black men using illegal firearms. The primary source of illegal guns is the theft or loss of licensed firearms, averaging 24 incidents daily. Despite women constituting only 11 percent of gun-related murder victims, firearms play a significant role in violence against women (VAW), especially in intimate partner femicides. Firearms also play a role in violence against LGBTQ+ individuals, and xenophobic attacks of non-South African blacks, with hate crimes disproportionately affecting these communities.

The South African Firearms Legislation

The process of enacting the FCA involved substantial input from civil society organizations, research institutions, and grassroots participation. In the years leading up to the FCA, the government initiated several committees to address the proliferation of firearms. This engagement disrupted the male-dominated discourse on firearms, emphasizing the collective good and promoting more inclusive policies. Several global, regional, and national developments influenced South Africa's firearms legislation. The UN Firearms Protocol negotiated concurrently with the FCA, adopted a law-enforcement approach to control firearms. Additionally, the UN Program of Action (PoA) recognized the role of civil society in small arms policy development, paving the way for discussions on the gendered nature and impacts of firearm-related violence.

Regionally, the Southern Africa Development Community's (SADC) Firearms Protocol reinforced South Africa's efforts to implement the FCA rigorously, aligning it with neighboring countries' more restrictive firearm legislation. Notably, these protocols lacked gender-specific provisions. Nationally, influential gun control movements in Canada, the UK, and Australia prompted policy changes. In Canada, background checks included spousal interviews to reduce the risk of violence against women. The UK and Australia also implemented firearm control measures following large-scale massacres. In all these cases, women-led alliances and civil society played pivotal roles in advocating for legislative reform.

Crafting, Passing, and Implementing the FCA

Policy formulation in South Africa follows two essential steps: the Green Paper, a preliminary policy document for public input, and the White Paper, which represents the final policy position. The Firearms Control Bill, approved by the cabinet, was published in late 1999 and presented to parliament in May 2000. During this period, the public was invited to submit written comments, leading to over 3,000 submissions, indicating significant public interest. Additionally, 93 oral submissions were made during public hearings in mid-2000. While firearm owners, predominantly white men, dominated the hearings, the Gun Control Alliance (GCA), representing diverse groups, including public health experts, researchers, religious communities, and young people from violence-affected communities, contributed significantly. During the final review of the Bill by the Portfolio Committee for Police (PCoP), there was resistance, even within the African National Congress (ANC), to include language-strengthening protections for women in their homes and reluctance to legislate interim protection orders as sufficient grounds for denying gun certificate applications. This advocacy included some measures to safeguard women, although only some of the complete set of proposals. This outcome influenced the prevailing cultural norms within the legislative sphere, emphasizing that the private domain should remain unlegislated.

Effects on Firearm-Related Deaths and Firearm Ownership

Over the last two decades in South Africa, the development and implementation of SALW control policies revealed a discernible pattern. The FCA significantly reduced firearm-related intimate femicides from 1999 to 2009. A ten-year retrospective study indicated a decline in women killed by their intimate partners, dropping from four women per day in 1999 to three per day in 2009, primarily due to reduced firearm-related fatalities. However, a surge in gun related incidences was observed from 2011. The recent surge in firearm-related violence is attributable to the breakdown of the national firearms control system. Poor enforcement and compliance have led to an increased availability of firearms. For example, 33 percent of licensed firearm owners failed to renew their licenses in 2015–16, yet these firearms remained in their possession. The firearms management system has also faced fraud, corruption, inadequate stockpile management, under-resourcing, and a lack of policing capacity.

Lessons From South Africa's Experience

The South African experience with crafting and implementing small arms control policies offers valuable insights for addressing gun violence and gender-based violence (GBV) in other countries. The FCA faced stiff opposition from deep historical and cultural connections to firearm ownership, especially among white men. However, a positive aspect of process is the growing influence of women's meaningful participation and leadership in an area traditionally dominated by men. South Africa has moved closer to a situation where all affected parties can contribute to shaping policies that enhance safety and security for everyone.

Case Study 4: Firearm Ownership in Serbia: A Gender Perspective

In the Republic of Serbia, like in many other places, women are the primary victims of gender-based and domestic violence. Available data indicate that firearms misuse is not gender-neutral; it impacts the lives of women and men differently, particularly in the context of domestic violence and intimate partner violence. Firearms are not solely used for homicides; they are also employed for intimidation, threats, psychological abuse, sexual violence, and exerting control over victims (UNDP Serbia, 2021).

In 2016, Serbia was home to approximately 618,061 registered firearms in civilian hands, with 23,539 owned by private legal entities (non-state entities). Although these figures show a significant decline from 2007, when it was estimated that Serbia harbored over two million firearms, they still underscore the presence of a substantial number of weapons. A substantial segment of Serbia's population legally possesses, carries, and uses firearms. Authorization extends beyond military and police personnel, encompassing members of various security agencies, customs officers, individuals involved in detective work, court guards, private security companies, forest guards, gamekeepers, and those managing hunting grounds. Thus, in 2016 alone, over 10,000 weapons were seized, with a mere 744 of them being illegally held. Additionally, 874 misdemeanor charges were filed for negligent weapon possession and use that year.

Setting the Legal Framework for Effective SALW Control

While some Serbian laws recognize the connection between firearms misuse and domestic violence and have contributed to reducing the number of homicides involving firearms, challenges persist, preventing complete and adequate protection. The reported domestic violence cases are increasing yearly, yet they represent only a fraction of the problem's accurate scale. When crimes are reported, over half of them are rejected due to insufficient evidence or victims' unwillingness to testify.

Working with its national partners, UNDP sought to reduce the risk of firearms misuse in the context of GBV. Its specific goals include improving legislative and strategic frameworks, enhancing prevention measures, and raising awareness among men, women, girls, and boys regarding the risks associated with firearm misuse.

Gendered Impact of Gun Violence

The undeniable correlation between firearms and GBV reveals a grim reality (UNDP Serbia, 2021). Women constitute about 64.2 percent of all victims killed by a family member, while men account for 35.8 percent.

Intimate Partner Attacks as Leading Cause of Murders

Intimate partners are responsible for 42.2 percent of murders committed within families, with women falling victim to their partners in 88.1 percent of cases, compared to 11.9 percent for men. In situations involving family members, 31.2 percent of these homicides involve firearms, and women represent 63.2 percent of victims killed by a family member with a firearm, in stark contrast to 36.8 percent for men. An overwhelming 91.1 percent of individuals killed by a partner wielding a firearm are women, with men comprising only 8.9 percent of such victims. Astonishingly, in cases of intimate partner violence, 39.4 percent of women are killed with a firearm, and a staggering 51.9 percent of GBV incidents involving firearms result in death. The likelihood of death due to firearms misuse in GBV cases is three times higher than in criminal contexts.

A Persisting Gun Culture

The persistence of a "gun culture" is a significant obstacle to combating Domestic Violence (DV), rooted in traditional values and citizens' mistrust of institutions. In Serbia, publicly available data from institutions providing precise insights into firearms misuse in the context of DV and GBV are lacking. The existing data and statistics, particularly those related to criminal offenses, are insufficiently informative and lack categories relevant to firearms misuse. Gender mainstreaming in firearms control necessitates dismantling the entrenched "gun culture" and associated gender roles in Serbia.

Weak Legal Framework for SALW Control

The legal framework governing firearm purchase, possession, and carrying, reasons for firearm confiscation, conditions for carrying service weapons, and firearm storage methods, among others, require a thorough analysis and potential improvement to prevent violence committed with firearms, DV, and GBV. Additionally, laws related to institutional responses to DV, GBV, and penal policies need redefinition, especially given the current leniency in DV cases. A strategic approach to strengthening the intersection between SALW and GBV is vital to facilitate collaboration among various entities dedicated to combating GBV.

Lesson from the Serbian SALW Control Case

1. Serbia's national documents predominantly adopt a protective approach, emphasizing the correlation between firearms and women's security and protection against violence. However, the process is not participatory, and data

and records on the relationship between GBV and firearms are grossly inadequate.

2.   Encouragingly, Serbia's National Action Plan for the implementation of Resolution 1325 aims to introduce a gender perspective into all public policies related to defense and security. It also seeks to improve the safety and security of women employed or engaged in the security sector and investigate and prevent violence against women effectively.

3.   Available data indicates that the probability of death due to the misuse of firearms in domestic violence cases is three times more common than incidents in a criminal context. Serbia ranked 17th out of 48 countries regarding female homicides involving firearms between 2007 and 2012. From 2012 to 2016, 84 homicides were committed with firearms, with 21 percent of victims being women. During the same period, 35 women and 186 men were injured by firearms.

4.   Serbia has established legal frameworks and regulations regarding firearm acquisition, possession, and carrying, with provisions addressing public safety and potential risks. However, the effective enforcement of these regulations, particularly regarding medical and psychological assessments, remains an ongoing challenge.

5.   The Law on Weapons and Ammunition, supplemented by relevant bylaws, regulates two critical conditions: physical fitness and the manner of firearm storage. However, there are several shortcomings:

> § The law does not include specific provisions to address emergencies related to domestic violence or protective measures against violence under family law as grounds for permit denial. Also,

§ The law lacks detailed provisions governing the behavior of firearm owners within their private spaces and does not establish protective measures or sanctions for owners disturbing family or household members.

§ The law does not specify the roles and duties of specialists and other health workers in providing information about patients authorized to own or carry firearms or regarding changes in their health conditions.

§ Security vetting procedures are outlined in the Law on Police but offer police officers discretion in selecting information sources. There is no obligation to consult family

members or investigate
dysfunctional family
relationships as in South
Africa's FCA.

CONCLUSION

This paper examines the critical issue of mainstreaming gender considerations in the control of small arms and light weapons (SALW). We explored the complex and multifaceted relationship between SALW and sexual and gender-based violence (SGBV), highlighting the urgent need to adopt a more inclusive approach in SALW control efforts. It is evident that the implications of mainstreaming gender in SALW control are far-reaching and of paramount importance. The global landscape of SALW is rife with conflict, violence, and suffering. These weapons often serve as catalysts for SGBV, disproportionately affecting women who find themselves at greater risk of experiencing violence when SALW are present. Thus, gender-sensitive policies and legislation are essential to address the distinctive vulnerabilities that women and men face in the context of SALW.

The case studies provided in Section 3 have shed light on the real-world applications of gender mainstreaming in SALW control. These studies have emphasized the importance of recognizing men as victims of SGBV and women as active participants in both conflict and support for SALW proliferation. Each case has revealed unique challenges and opportunities, underscoring that a one-size-fits-all approach to gender mainstreaming is not feasible. Instead, it is imperative that such efforts are context-specific and consider the broader socio-political and cultural dynamics at play. We have also witnessed the critical role that gender-sensitive legislation and regulation play in preventing and addressing SGBV related to SALW. Gender-responsive training for security forces and relevant stakeholders is equally vital, ensuring that the proper mechanisms are in place to identify and respond to instances of violence. Moreover, this paper has highlighted the need for comprehensive data collection and research that takes into account the differing experiences and needs of women and men.

In essence, mainstreaming gender in SALW control is not only a matter of compliance with international norms but a moral and strategic imperative. It is crucial for achieving comprehensive, just, and lasting peace. Hence the need for a paradigm shift, moving beyond the traditional security-focused approach to SALW control and toward a more holistic perspective that recognizes the gender-specific impacts of these weapons.

We conclude by emphasizing that the journey toward mainstreaming gender in SALW control is ongoing and requires the collaboration of governments, international organizations, civil society, and communities. By integrating gender considerations into policies, legislation, and training, we can build a world where the devastating impacts of SALW are mitigated, where SGBV is reduced, and where the principles of justice, equity, and peace are upheld.

As we move forward, human societies must remain committed to the vision of a world where the control of SALW is not only about disarmament but also about addressing the gender-specific challenges and injustices that have long been associated with these lethal tools. It is our hope that the insights presented in this paper will inspire further research, dialogue, and, most importantly, concrete actions that lead us closer to this shared vision of a safer and more inclusive world.

REFERENCES

Bastick, M. (n.d.). Integrating Gender in Post-Conflict Security Sector Reform. Geneva Centre for the Democratic Control of Armed Forces (DCAF) Policy Paper – №29. https://www.dcaf.ch/sites/default/files/publications/documents/pp29.pdf

Bonn International Center for Conversion. (n.d.). Brief 24: Gender Perspectives on Small Arms and Light Weapons: Regional and International Concerns. https://www.bicc.de/uploads/tx_bicctools/brief24.pdf

Conaway, C. P. (2012). Small Arms, Light Weapons and Landmines. Inclusive Security. https://www.inclusivesecurity.org/wp-content/uploads/2012/04/48_small_arms.pdf

International Action Network on Small Arms. (2021, September 20). Strengthening the Connection Between Small Arms and Light Weapons Controls and the Women, Peace, and Security Agenda. https://iansa.org/wp-content/uploads/2021/10/Strengthening-the-Connection-Between-Small-Arms-and-Light-Weapons-Controls-and-the-Women-Peace-and-Security-Agenda-ENGLISH.pdf

Joshi, S. R. (n.d.). Global Governance to Address Proliferation of Small Arms and Light Weapons to Prevent Armed Conflicts and Promote Peace. Ideas for Peace. https://ideasforpeace.org/content/global-governance-to-address-proliferation-of-small-arms-and-light-weapons/

LeBrun, E. (Ed.). (2019). Gender-responsive Small Arms Control: A Practical Guide. Small Arms Survey, Graduate Institute of International and Development Studies, Geneva.

https://smallarmssurvey.org/sites/default/files/resources/SAS-GLAS S-Gender-HB.pdf

North Atlantic Treaty Organization. (n.d.). NATO Guidelines for Gender Mainstreaming in Small Arms & Light Weapons Projects. https://salw.hq.nato.int/Content/resources/NGforGM_EN_Small%2 0Arms.pdf

Organization for Security and Co-operation in Europe (OSCE). (n.d.). Arms Control. https://www.osce.org/arms-control

Reaching Critical Will of the Women's International League for Peace and Freedom. (2016). Preventing Gender-Based Violence Through Arms Control: Tools and guidelines to implement the Arms Trade Treaty and UN Programme of Action. United Nations. https://att-assistance.org/sites/default/files/2019-01/rcw_att-unpoa-g ender-based-violence.pdf

South Eastern and Eastern Europe Clearinghouse for the Control of Small Arms and Light Weapons (SEESAC). (2018). Gender and SALW: Gender Aspects of SALW and How to Address Them in Practice. https://www.seesac.org/f/docs/Gender-and-Security/Gender-Aspects -of-SALW---ENG-28-09-2018.pdf

United Nations. (2006). Women, Gender and DDR. https://www.unddr.org/modules/IDDRS-5.10-Women-Gender-and-D DR.pdf

United Nations. (2022). The Sustainable Development Goals Report 2022. https://unstats.un.org/sdgs/report/2022/The-Sustainable-Developme nt-Goals-Report-2022.pdf

United Nations Development Programme. (2022). UNDP 10-Point Action Agenda for Advancing Gender Equality in Crisis Settings. https://www.undp.org/sites/g/files/zskgke326/files/2022-11/UNDP-10-Point-Action-Agenda-for-Advancing-Gender-Equality-in-Crisis-Settings.pdf

UNDP Serbia. (2021, August 27). Small arms and light weapons, gender-based violence and domestic violence: analysis of regulatory framework and practice. https://www.undp.org/serbia/publications/small-arms-and-light-weapons-gender-based-violence-and-domestic-violence-analysis-regulatory-framework-and-practice

United Nations Institute for Disarmament Research (UNIDR). (2020). Gender Perspectives In Arms Control And Disarmament: Views From Africa: Workshop Report. https://unidir.org/sites/default/files/2020-05/Gender%20Perspectives%20in%20Arms%20Control%20and%20Disarmament%20-%20Views%20from%20Africa.pdf

United States Institute of Peace. (n.d.). Gender, War & Peacebuilding: A Study Guide Series on Peace and Conflict for Independent Learners and Classroom Instructors. https://www.usip.org/sites/default/files/files/NPECSG12.pdf

United Nations Office for Disarmament Affairs (UNODA). (n.d.). Gender and Small Arms Control. https://disarmament.unoda.org/gender-and-small-arms-control/

United Nations Office on Drugs and Crime (UNODC). (2020). Gender Brief for UNODC Staff: Mainstreaming gender in Organized Crime & Illicit Trafficking projects. https://www.unodc.org/documents/Gender/Thematic_Gender_Briefs_English/Org_crime_and_trafficking_brief_23_03_2020.pdf

United Nations Population Fund (UNPFA). (2002). The Impact of Armed Conflict on Women and Girls: A Consultative Meeting on Mainstreaming Gender in Areas of Conflict and Reconstruction, Bratislava, Slovakia, 13–15 November 2001. https://www.unfpa.org/sites/default/files/pub-pdf/impact_conflict_women.pdf

UN Women. (n.d.). Facts and Figures: Women, Peace, and Security. https://www.unwomen.org/en/what-we-do/peace-and-security/facts-and-figures

Watson, C. (2022, October 13). Militarizing Gender or Humanizing Small Arms Control? Global Observatory. https://theglobalobservatory.org/2022/10/militarizing-gender-or-humanizing-small-arms-control/